A LAST HIKE IN

ISBN: 979-8-218-15861-3

A LAST HIKE IN

poems
Peter Weltner

MARRROWSTONE PRESS / SEATTLE

For Atticus
for Music

and with thanks to

Galen Garwood

Clarinda Harris

Patricia McCarthy

and

Robert Mohr

Table of Contents

I

II

III

IV

I

More Worlds than This One

1.

It's a ceremonious, stately old forest, the brush dense,
trees pocked with lichen, moss-covered, the canopy
so thick the sky's invisible. The quiet eloquence
of morning woods, cold from winds off the sea,
the dew-wet bark pungent, roots' smelling of musk
and mildew. Willows bow low to the shallow creek
winding among them, their spindly branches dusk-
hued in a humanly moody forest. Wild flowers' petals speak
silently, in whispers, flittering, spinning, gliding
on a stream that flows without motion, without singing,
voiceless as last patches of snow melting in shadows.
A faint mist is looming over the summit above the tree
line, like a cerecloth veiling rocks and boulders, the sage-
and hyssop-colored, quartz-glittering, massive promontory
that seems to be always aspiring, climbing higher toward language.

2.

This far from cities, the world is spared mankind's pollution
spared mortality, too, one might say, the air balmy,
fragrant with spruce, fir, beech, the sun steady,
blessing with its sweetness leaves as they ripen,
its light motionless in the heavens as if ordered by
the gods not to move for a moment, the birds
tranquil as statues. No bushes, trees rustle. Try
to be as quiet. Try to find in its silence the words
you need to speak of the unwilled beauty of creation
even as you cry for yourself and more worlds than this one.

3.

Hölderlin: "Their quieted hearts were filled with a silent
contentment and, as from the beginning,
alone, desire was satisfied. So be observant.
Such is man if fortune proves true by granting
its gifts to you who see and understand none

of it. You who must suffer, be brave, too, atone
for what's done. Then may you name the beloved
things with words rooted like trees, images that bud
and blossom like wild flowers in ancient woods that pain
you with what they know of beauty as you head in, tread deeper in."

Friendship

Curious, isn't it, how easy it is to say, "The Ground
of Being," and not know what it means. Two photos
of you I've kept help me remember. Time leaves
behind, as it moves ever onward, the haunting sound
of voices missed whispering with a music that glows
like cool jazz, you said, like clouds at night. What grieves
me most about our lost talks are the earth, people
you loved who are ghosts now, too, forests chopped, toppled,
depopulated. There's a burning, crackling in my head
like buildings on fire, a church smoking from its steeple.
You, my philosopher friend, my preacher, teacher,
propounder of profundities. Volatile. A staunch believer
in God, you'd insist, then laugh at me, at yourself,
for what we knew ought not be true, you, your bookshelf
of Athenian tragedies. Talk as philosophy, our words like an onrushing river.

I yearn for a world over the sea, a peerless, unafraid
city, paradisal, peaceful. You are a shade who has made
plain to me often since you died, "Death is no disaster,"
by which I suppose you mean you flow like water
or roam in woods as if time were a wilderness free
as a mountain you would climb to build on its summit
a house made of stone, no monument, just a space
to dwell in before you depart for some other place,
far stranger than the one we're born into. Where could it
be, save in the missing, missing, missing of life? To be
grounded somehow? It is the last day of the year. I don't mind
admitting I'm growing more confused by calendars. Some find
them imposing and hang them on a door, the important
times before them circled as I circle yours–the date
I always mark first, the one on which you left, disappeared
for good somehow–whenever I pin a new one to a wall.

                              I've feared
death too long, my wandering buddy, my half-mad friend. Rome,

I agreed, should prove a fine place to die in. That is, if by 'home'
you had intended to cite a classical beginning. I live by the sea,
ancient Greek, in a way, like the shores of unknowing you showed me.
My confusion is all I can offer to greet you there. This plea disguised as a poem.

Mohawk Valley

1.

On the way is the obvious, a trail up a hill
to a clearing overlooking the Mohawk
Valley, the sky icy blue in the chill
morning air, a few cirrus clouds chalk
white and floating slowly out of sight.
The leaves gleam crimson, rust, golden,
fleshy orange, lemon rind in a last rite
of late October, like tapestries woven
with no pattern, as if spontaneous, free,
random, the light they emanate bright
as a kaleidoscope's without its geometry.
In a remote grove of spruce and hickory,
a rivulet from yesterday's rains trickles
through weeds, over roots, rocks, and twigs.

A fat gray squirrel ponders the nuts the hickories
have dropped near it and with its paws digs
in the earth, gnaws one, climbs an oak. Half-
hidden in a thicket, a red fox sniffs, suspecting
human presence, frozen as a photograph
until it scampers through leaves, bushes rustling
at its flight. Spruce and hickory, gray
squirrel, red fox, a rivulet circling a boulder:
all must, as soon as tomorrow or the day
after, like fall's leaves' embers that smolder
below first snows, succumb to winter. Say
what you see tells the whole story, everything
you need to know or to comprehend about what
it means. That you are either within it or nowhere: not this, but that.

2.

Imagine the words you're reading are a frigid, icy white
field glazed with frost one late morning,
its drooping flowers faded to brown, a bite

in the dying autumn air, leaves clutching
the ground in rotting, scattered piles,
as a man (a truth-seeker he might call
himself) climbs over fences and stiles
round a meadow to a graveyard wall
where the buried are said to be resurrected,
or so he has been told though left
to wonder, too, if the awakened dead are led
somewhere obscure to the living, bereft
though they are, voices from the night refuting the old
conundrum that in language the sun never sets, yet burns stone cold.

3.

The hilly fields on which the staunch trees stand
roll like waves in an October storm, shaking
their trunks and limbs. This is a wind-blown land
in autumn that, without protesting,
bears the great, ponderous weight of your
hidden, yet to be lived life upon it, earth,
sky, soul rendered plainly visible this hour
by twilight's setting fire to the worth
of the world as you have known it, trees' leaves
and branches, all the Mohawk Valley, ignited
by sunset. Beside their own deaths, what grieves
people most is the death of their friends. Poetry's
no use, nor their once passionate muscles and blood,
nor all they'd beheld long enough at last to have understood.

4.

The mind's woods are stripped bare for us, it is claimed, for our solitary
contemplation, heavy snow a blank, windowless white outside
with nothing for us to hear or see, no October beauty to sustain us, where mercy
arrives only to strain all laws of sense, unable to justify all the good that has died.

Do we become the silence that dwells within us, the ineffable, unspeakable
extremity of unknowing, the wound of which the mystics write
as a manifestation of God's absence, the corporeal, palpable
denial of meaning, the howl that cries like wolves in the northern winter night?

I remember as a boy believing (this is near nonsense, this trivial, bitter
little story–though in a way it tells the truth of the first religious hurt
I felt) that, grown old, I would at last know enough to assert
myself, be free not of suffering, but of never knowing what it means, that sooner
or later I would have the language for it, plain and ordinary. If the world is everything
that is the case, why isn't its silence sufficient to listen to, why can't I stop thinking?

5.

Recently, or maybe for the first time, I read
the story of the Valley of the Seven
Turns and found that what it said
told of life's end as if it were a fixed season,
late autumn or early winter, say, on
a snowy Mount Narayama. The hour
comes when fat crows must devour
the dying old man. Strapped in a chair,
he grasps his carrier's strong shoulders
without glancing back or straining
to see the looming mountain peaks ahead
where winds are blowing too hard to dare
another step. Yet he knows where he is going:
through wilderness and a haunted forest, up trails,
steep and rocky, to where every word he's learned fails
him as he lies and waits for death to come like birds among black boulders.

Ribbon Dance

1.

The moon is a rubbery, pale
ball bulging above
a tree-lined horizon

as it rises swift as a boat full sail
out of
the dragon-

green, slick-scaled canopy
toward a sunset
whose reds, lavenders, yellows

burn this beautifully
only at twilight. A duet
between swallows, slow

and lovely, fades as the trees
darken
into silhouettes

and butterflies, beetles, bees
begin
as the sun sets

to give way to moths, locust, crickets
while the trees' leaves,
twigs, limbs

are threaded like webs or fishermen's nets,
whatever weaves
the world together, as old hymns

do sometimes, letting the eye
see
why night's lucidity can be clearer than day's,

offering to teach us how to die
by the light
of sundown, showing us how a fading world prays.

2.

At noon in the park,
August
burns the leaves

and grass dark
as iron rust,
deceives

your keenest sight with
its brightness,
sunlight clouded by dust.

For the fifth
day, the press
of each new gust

of wind makes it hard
to breathe,
becomes oppressive,

as if the spirit, too, is scarred
by heat. Bequeath
what you will to heaven. Give

it everything, deny it nothing.
When the sky
grows too bright

to contemplate, earthly life loses its meaning,
the sun-stunned eye
mis-led by its blinding light like a hawk in flight.

3.

Another year is turning as a hard wind
blows gulls, crows
swallows into the loops and leaps of a Chinese

ribbon dance. The mind
is what it briefly knows
despite all it leaves

behind. The birds flap their wings,
test their strength
against the air's,

unable to fly anywhere far, only in rings
the width
of a stream the moon glares

down upon, its pale light rippling in its urgent water
while night birds, like children playing,
are making

a game of it, as if elated by redwood, spruce, fir,
eucalyptus shaking, rustling, shivering
at the end of day, fast dissolving,

into shade and shadow, the birds twirling with the flare
of old souls dancing,
as if in the swirl of their delight in flying they understand everything.

Cattails

The unmediated, thoughtless beauty of things. On the ocean that summer
morning, a school of mackerel was skimming the surface while the sky's
dawn-borne fog was the mottled gray of gutter-tossed, rain-soaked newspaper.
I'm remembering Chris on our last night while he slept in his t-shirt and Levis

and where we'd hiked the next day, the scrub brush on cliffs bent eastward
from the surge of winds off the sea while fist-sized rocks suddenly
dislodged and plummeted onto a deserted beach. And the narrow, sandy ford
we'd crossed a stream on as it trickled through reeds and rushes. Covered by

hip-tall, sun-tanned golden grasses, the rolling hill we'd hiked up. The snake-
skin black, dilapidated barn we'd watched slowly sloughing off its peeling scales
of rotted wood onto the poppy fields in the meadow below. Moments shadowed
by the flickering of love, like otters sunning, frolicking in the mud of the Russian
River.

By late afternoon, we'd reached the estuary, fogged in, as the high tide flowed   ·
in like a flood. Is it true once the earth has spoken, it makes no mistakes?
The froth fierce waves spilled on the beach looked white as cotton, as the cattails'
bursting into seeds, floating in wetlands misty from the heat, that last day of summer.

Journey's End

Ours is a long sea journey like that of birds that fly
at night guided only by stars. Deserts.
Pinnacles. Alder, birch forests. Then a spring
at the end of it. A steep descent from high
country where streams wash clean the hurts
of a lifetime. Both of our faces are fading
fast. Thatch houses, cold hearths, their thousand
bare rooms where we search, as if each is alone,
to find one restful enough to lie beside
each other again in the silence of an alien land.
Stand by me on a rocky shore near stone
caves carved out of cliffs before a forbiddingly wide
sea, waiting for a ship that will never show. Come.
Stay by me always as together we walk the long, hard way home.

Eclipse

Night in the bat-eyed sight
of it, owl-eared sound
of it, dew-hungry grasses'
desire for the sweet taste

of it, the fight of breezes
and wind to win from air
the pure smell of it,
more translucent than water,

more cool and bracing. The spell of it,
to walk freely, incarnate,
lost in its unlit gloom
but unafraid of the loss

that day is. Never to balk at it,
never to dread it. In the park,
a lone coyote howls
at its desolation, a cantillation

born from the beauty of it,
its dark finer than dark's
is, elusive as music.
Tonight, I see you alive

in its full obscurity, ours
what night has become,
not frightening but real
as our shadows are, reminders

of passions long passed, as once
we were, lovers eclipsed,
crying out in ecstasy, turned
cat, raccoon, nightingale, firefly.

Filling Station

Gathered against the hard rain inside Ben Caudle's
Texaco station, five men, friends, all farmers
wearing soaked bib overalls, t-shirts, muddy
galoshes, sprawl on benches by display racks
of Tube Rose snuff, Camels, and Sen-Sen powders
while eating a lunch of vienna sausages, pimento cheese
sandwiches and RC Colas, watching fields out back
being washed away. It's been raining all summer,
a steady deluge every day, a tempest that leaves
behind only sterile clay and stones and sharp rocks,
the last good soil blackening streams and rivers.
Their eyes look blank and unsurprised, no resistance
left in them. No one is listening to the radio, its news
of the war, preachers promising miracle cures. Silence
is like loneliness, isn't it? The pain of it, though no one knows whose.

II

Ten Ancient Greek Fragments on War

1.

Let neighbor compete with neighbor,
pursue greater riches. Discord
befits mankind.

Let potter hate potter. Let poets bore
each other to fury. Who can afford
peace? The best on the worst have always dined.

Get drunk on the blood of the fawn
you tore with your claws.
Be a lion stalking prey, sure

of your strength. Trace the light of dawn
as it fills the hills. Follow jackdaws
and swallows in flight. Be pure

in pursuit as hungry birds. Mount the tower shown
you and sack its town.
Grab the reins of your steeds

and ride the royal car you lead. All that's known
is this, says Ares. What you've sown
you've never sown enough of to feed off others' greed.

2.

Shepherds, threshers, farmers gossip about
kings and dismal weather,
complain of chill summer rains

on what was to be a fruitful morning, shout
out loud when alone together
about what little of their labor remains

from what was taken for the soldiers who long for
lamb like them, figs, melons, pine
nuts, sweet juice of pomegranate,

as if the days ahead might greet them like a lover
in their beds, like a god entering a shrine,
face shining, omen of a happier fate.

3.

Mens' souls evaporate in winds
that blow them away
easily as mullein seeds in spring.

Eternal night's power blinds
us all, betrays
us, its beating

wings lifting us higher until our souls drift
in the air like boats
at sea by ragged storms from wars unmoored.

4.

You give your precious, hard-earned gift,
sheeps' throats
cut, wine poured

for Hades. What is there left for you to say,
Adrastos? You hear the din
of clashing soldiers

ravaging Troy, near or far away,
among them your kin.
As the fallen city burns and smolders,

you say. "I have watched my siblings
kill or be killed,
each a patriot, each a warrior.

Whoever bears witness also sings,
if he is skilled
in threnody,

but how can tragedy
speak of pity
for those of us who see

everything yet can do nothing but suffer,
like the soul of Homer
chanting his poetry."

5.

According to the Fabulae of Hyginus
Aether, the light
of heaven,

is the son of Chaos
and Night,
though his genealogy is uncertain.

Aether and Day are the parents of Caelus
the sky, Terra the earth, Mare,
the sea, and Terra and Aether together

by incest are the parents of fighting and fear, of Tartarus,
of Alecto, Megaera, Tisiphone,
the three furies: war, vengeance, anger.

6.

Hector, hero of heroes, your bones
rest in a golden urn
shrouded by a soft purple cloth

laid deep in a deep grave with a heap
of great stones to raise the mound.
Tonight we post guards

to ensure against Achaean attacks. More stones
raise the barrow. We yearn
for you to return, mourn for Ilion, like a moth

at night that flits at your expiring flame.   Keep
watch on us. The wings of birds fluttering, the ghostly sounds
you hear in the dark are our funereal rites, the paeans of bards.

7.

Mycenae destroyed signifies no more than driftwood
or seaweed twisted into knots of rags,
or a white stone, flat

and red-veined, but of no value, no good,
no use to anyone. Stags
leap over the mountains.   What first begat

the kingdom's fate? A deer, is it Iphigenia?, stares
in a river,
then leaps over a crevasse,

escaping. Whenever history dares
to rationalize disaster, more slaughter
follows, the bloodied plains, the ravaged palaces.

8.

At the Hot Gates, their city shamed
when they were late for Marathon,
Leonidas and his leather skinned

men stand in line on rocky ground
between stark cliffs, Spartan
fighters commanding the road Persians

must pass to win the war. Penetrating as the sound
of an aulos, they chant a ritual ode
to taunt their enemies, boast, goad

them into battle: three hundred soldiers,
lovers of men, salvaging their city's reputation
standing side by side, naked but armed, awaiting invasion.

9.

You, no friend to mortals, allow
youth to blossom, to flame
brighter, Ares.

War god, with your war strength, show
us how to bring fame
to our city by making peace.

Expel bitter memories from our heads.
No longer provoke us into
the bone-cold hatred

of battle. Our hearths are warm, our herds
fed, our crops thriving. Few
are our days. Let them be blessed.

Listen, my love. Here is a poem
I found in a scroll of Greek
epitaphs at first light this morning:

"If you say nothing, Diodoros,
you speak to me my name.
My days are nights in an endless winter.

Light your lamp. By its flame, in the toil
of its burning, see why I cannot sleep.
Glaze your chest and arms with oil."

10.

An oak grove, like a temple's marble columns,
casting night's last shadows.
Distant as muffled, thrumming drums,
waves roll in, breaking far below. Foes
no longer foes. Enemies no more enemies.
Mist thin clouds,
linen-pale. Crickets singing, cicadas' summer sounds,
birds testing new harmonies,
new worlds to fly to. A girl opens shutters to dry her hair
in the warmth of late dawn. The ground
of being, found
in the everyday, in her care-
free beauty. She's spying on a boy in a plain tunic
staring at another with myrtle eyes. Their watchful music.
Plaited like curtains, translucent as alabaster, limestone cliffs
shimmer as a soft wind blows
off the sea. More shutters open. A gull drifts
on its currents. Morning's brightening shadows
fall from olive trees gleam-
ing in the heat. Say the day is a snake

sunning its back. An auspicious dream.

A noon moon shining on a deep blue lake.

Light as joy. As concord's splendor.

Minute by minute, hour after hour,

time sleeps

dreamily by a stream that feeds it. It is our

day.   No reed or lyre grieves. No one weeps

or mourns. This peace we've declared in our bed, the end to our war.

Water Man Fire Dream

for Robert Mohr

1.

Fifty years ago, in summer, the heavens flared one morning
as we woke early in our bed to a sun at dawn
that had risen gray and tawny while hiding
behind clouds, then suddenly broke free as if drawn
up by the sky's desire for more radiance, eager
to embrace its swelling, sweltering light. Think of Helios, driver
of his blazing chariot and four horses, of the sea
into which his child fell. Fire, water. Mythology
confounds them in one story, sun and sea alive,
timeless in the way that myths all strive to be—
archaic languages, ancient images that survive, thrive
in the oldest memories that burn within us. The absolute
of ecstasy eludes us. Yet we pray for passion's keenest joy to be
eternal. For what is absolute if not that transcendent matter of human artistry,
like an undying tree, branches and leaves, trunk and root.

Picture an oak grove, noble as a temple's marble columns,
that casts a long night's fading shadows on us where
wind-blown trees sound like muted drums
rumbling, waves breaking like thunder. We feel no care
for tomorrow, safe inside, lying in bed together
after a night of love-making. A neighbor's barking
dog stirs us fully awake as we hold one another,
tighter, unwilling to let go of the hours just passed. Lovers
rejoice in sensualities. Years after, I see you drying
your hair, smiling at me with your blue, wide-awake eyes,
standing naked in a doorway as outside the day shines on trees
so intently their leaves gleam like olives while, wafted by breezes
rippling like currents in a stream, flocks of birds drift, circle as if it pleases
them to fly aimlessly as I gaze at your body wishing it might stay unchanging
like a torso in an ancient marble frieze.

2.

I am old. Twilight smolders like wild fires dying on a mountain peak.
Dreams slip out my bedroom while night floods in.
Shining through my window, the moon shames me. "Speak
to me," it says, "confess to me that when
your lover left, you refused to listen
to my consolations." "How much longer
must I bear it?," I replied. "I've grown too old, in cold weather,
reliving the years when
we were together. Before he went, he told me (yes, on the shore of a lake
made starless, moonless by a sky
shrouded in clouds), my dear friend, the kind, beautiful man
for whose sake
I cannot betray what we were together, he said, who every night in bed would lie
beside me under moonlight, "Someday you'll be at peace with it,
                                    someday you'll understand."

And I do understand, though separation is indifferent to its necessity,
how, even justified, it stupefies
the mind with an impunity
that defies
accepting the reasons for it. Searching daily,
I walk the beach.   Today, I saw a crow peck at the carcass
of a gull. (How it bloodies
the sands of my thoughts still.) Fish heads, crab shells, lay in dune grass
where ravenous ravens ripped at seal's blubber, its pearly lard dappled
by sea foam. Bleached to rubbery gray, its hide was peeled,
stripped, swallowed.
                        Stretched out on a bed of seaweed, does it
dream of paradise, flesh no more, its bones beak-etched, slit,
broken, then transfigured into scrimshaw, as if silenced by mortality
every creature's needful, implacable desires cry out in despair, "Remember me."

3.

I dream of north coast woods in midwinter, icy
slick green moss and weeds.
No trails to follow. Needles, leaves: tree
limb after tree limb tangled together. Seeds
dormant in muddy ground. A pallid sky,
a forest in shadows, sunlight
like a bit of a half-recalled song or lines of poetry,
oak groves formidable as night
snow on twigs and brush flickering like stars
or moonlight shining off water:
intimations,
of how desire is a wilderness, the danger
of hiking through a forest stripped of foliage
toward a lake with a dock and a boat we'd embark on to voyage
beyond an island that's bleak, solid as a massive boulder,
with its jagged rocks scattered
along a shore blanched by snow cover,
blue-tinted ice floes floating past. I watch a rowboat sea-battered
by waves high and rough,
in which two men at the oars, barely
visible, sail. How hard, tough
it is to fish these waters, cold and icy
day after day, the catch thin,
the constant chill
in their bones. How difficult it is to begin
again wondering if it is worth the risk, the repetitive drill,
the endless challenge of another winter
spent trekking through woods, trying to find you, pining to surrender.

4.

All these many years later I can still smell,

feel, taste you on my fingers. Sweat and seed

mingled with saliva.

I could not always tell

which was yours, which mine, freed

by love from needing to choose.

Some of your clothes

still hang in my closet. The music

you'd favored plays in my head.

Who else knows

now how good we were together?

How handsome and classic?

The Greeks were right to be frightened

by their gods,

Eros most of all.

But tragedy is not

solely pathos and anguish,

but an ecstasy of anticipation

at what the Furies reborn as the Kind Ones might do.

How intensely our past haunts me, goes

wherever I go, pursued not only by the ordinary

things you'd left in our bedroom—the books, black

boots, sweatshirt, faded white briefs,

jacket that bring you back

to me—but by what in dreams lingers of pleasures

that are beyond the powers

of a poem's deliberate

images and rhymes and measures

to speak of.

Anarchic time.

I will tell you again the dream

I had of our first night.

How on a mountain in Lesvos

I found a shard of a kouros
and fell in love with it at first sight.
How I kissed its lips, sun-warm and inviting.
How your blood quickened. Why I feared nothing.

    5.

Rocks and vines drip drip like a broken faucet.
At the precipice of a sheer cliff, a stream
flows into a waterfall. It is near sunset.
Wind-shaken leaves sparkle like earrings, gleam

brighter as light fades. The waterfalls surge crash
onto the beach. Like a Mycenaean, you
stand at the edge of a grove, picking olives,
stash more into your bulging pockets. A green band

of leaves form a wreath, a crescent round your head
like a crown of laurel and bay. Stone walls.
Iron gates. Gold masks. Carved lions. See? Instead
of loss, I translate our past into legend. Ancient halls,

their bronze doors. You shiver in a seaborne chill,
your face like a marble statue's near a fountain
at the foot of a mountain that wine would fill
as abundantly as streams teem after long rain.

Hazy brush. Outcrop filmy with mist. Vines.
A dusk woven with gold strands. A palace threaded
with twilight. Who offers the rites, who dines
at this feast? Our bodies. Our minds. Beauteous. Wedded.

6.

Show us how each hour endures forever, Sun,
blazes by night and by day. Be proof,
as we seek it, of our paradise won.
Gold is your temple, beryl its roof.

Let sunset be dawn's birth, the first
the last. Let each creature end
where creation began, thirst
and hunger what love shall suspend.

I speak of ecstasy. The night bursts into flames.
Out of joy, our bodies say our names
as one together. While ships' lights turn
seas into conflagrations, our desires, like torches, burn.

7.

Snapshots are mirrors that, like memories, we pass
through to the other side where the past presides.
I look at him lovingly in the few snaps I have
of him and don't regret any of it, celebrate even
the few painful times. His short's waistband is
leaf green, his jeans the gray of the rock he stands
on, his sweat sparkling with the amber colored dust
we kicked up fast as we raced for the summit.
At his best friend's wedding, he looks natty
in his tux, his hands tucked in pockets, his black
patent leather shoes spit shiny, his pale blue
eyes bleary from last night's beery hot tub.
Taken in our apartment, he waits naked, the shades
drawn on us, his body glowing ever more numinous as twilight fades.

8.

Sixteen, I jackknifed off a board, hit my skull
on a rock in mud. The last thing I saw was
the sun, the lake I was drowning in clear as air.
Water man fire dream. Wiping a mirror clean
of steam after a shower, dripping, erect, he
drops his towel. A full moon rises onto our bed
on which, in the underwater room, he strokes
my cock. Just over our heads, crests break.
White water wind. The surface ripples in lunar
light, pale as a fire's last ashes, the cinders
too hot to touch. Desire is a torch that blazes
brightest when submerged, however dark the sea
I dive to him in. Water is freedom. Water is peace.
In the deep, gold gleams brighter than fire. But best of all things is water.

Crab Boats

Under worn-inner-tube gray clouds, an end of day
blue breaking through, the boats back
on the ocean sail out of the bay one
by one. Later, from a dune off The Great Highway,
I count five floating on a wide black
patch of sea beneath a foggy horizon.
The crew turn the deck lanterns on, making ready
for the night, preparing
for work. Far down, crabs begin to explore the traps.
The catch isn't what it used to be,
of course, but the men still sail out, hoping
for better, guided as ever by charts and maps.
As soon as they're caught the crabs will be piled in bins or buckets
filled with sea water to keep them alive, untangled from traps or nets.

The crabbers' boats risk the ocean's edge as strong
winds sweep sand off the beach onto dunes.
Their torch-like lights, mirrored by the sea,
burn like searchlights most of the long
night.
        In my mind's eye, I see birds, swans or loons,
supple, graceful, lovely,
flying across an ocean to a lake where they dive
in, lit by the moon, as if they'd been new born
out of the sky, weightless as the foam
from waves, to float free where they might thrive
like souls in paradise with nothing more to mourn
for in their songs. Like fiery spirits come home,
their wet feathers flare, in the night seeming to blaze even brighter
like these boats glowing like small suns in the dark as if their flames were fed by water.

2.

It is morning, a week after. Blocks of cement, torn up foundations
lie like boulders on the sand, battered
by waves--breakwaters, bastions
against high tides useless as rubble, tossed and scattered.
After a late night storm scared off the last crabber,
a green-gray cast glistens off the water
as from the eyes of a bird or cat.
A cast off crab lies dead on the beach, not fat
enough to have kept to sell, its claws, threaded, stringy
from seaweed and sea slick,
desperately clenched,
clinging to nothing, its hard, beady
eyes imploring, protruded,
bulging like an agèd man's, staring at the sky when he's mortally sick.

Yet, last night, until the late storm intensified
into a tempest forcing them back to port, I saw five
crab boats burning as if lit on fire, as if deified,
five golden-coin-like suns mimicking sunset, each a live
flame aligned upon the horizon,
the wind-threshed
plain they lay upon
smoldering until the sea beneath them
seemed to catch on fire, too: five suns wheeling on the rim
of the world, burning, burning
as if they were the beginning of a new universe
I had been given a vision
of, in whose black-as-a-hearse-
and-rider night sky five suns blazed never to die but westward rising.

An August Storm

An August storm. Tree-lined hills unlit
by stars or moon as rains fill a pit
quarried for stone, the water gray
as slate, dark as a cave by day,
black as death by night.   Like a wide crack or slit

in the earth, the mine seems to have split
itself open as if to submit
to the emptiness of heaven the way
an August storm

revels in disaster. None of life's pieces fit
together. Though a tempest can't quit
its thrilling display
of wind, hail, lightning, must humanity prey
on itself to stay true to the earth, the raging spirit
of an August storm?

The Epic Imagination

1.

A thousand fires were set on beaches
to proclaim the victory they had won
as they sailed home to Greece, torches
flaming brighter than dawn's sun

as it broke over the harbor. An old
rhapsode strummed his lyre and sang
of heroes as they stepped, bold
and arrogant, back on shore, no pang

in their hearts for the thousands lost
before the trick of the horse, the wooden
statue Epeius built to hold a host
of warriors, disguised as a peace offering–

mane, shank, loin, a votive beast placating
Zeus, Ares in a ruse that would bring
ruin to Troy. You know the story.
Why now repeat it, its incitement to history's

ceaseless mourning? Torches like beacons
on towers swept round ramparts
where mobs saluted them. As sunset's embers
linger to ignite dawn's light, so do cities

blaze from fires lit by their enemies,
incited by hatred into orgies
of destruction that history glorifies
in, the victories it praises, the warriors'

triumphs it champions, the passions
that emblazon poems and the stories
of men made hard and pitiless
by their glorious and conflagrant hearts.

2.

Three weary soldiers squabble over two leather bags
with only a few nuts and dates left in them, food
they've gathered on their long trek home. Cats,
sacred to Ailuros, sniff the blood
from oozing wounds, rags
from tunics stripped off dead men
used as bandages, cats hissing, ravenous as rats
gnawing on bones like the starving souls of the soldiers they'd beaten.

But how calm the Aegean is today, placid
as a lake while mirroring
the dawn that has just begun,
its light splendid,
yet blinding to look upon, like a Trojan's armor reflecting
the beaten gold leaf of the shield of an avenging Greek warrior's sun.

3.

Startled by war's profligacy,
brutality, peonies, irises,
azaleas,
lilies, astilbes, too,

trunks of oaks, their moss-covered stumps
verdurous as new grass,
birdsong
at the rumbling of distant drums:

all hide as when a new spring storm comes
to wash fall's rain-sodden
rotting leaves
deeper into mud. Two soldiers hike

through woods where long-tusked boars are hunted
and under every flat, heavy stone
lie like a secret
living things retreating from sunlight,

beetle or scorpion
waiting to sting
if freed, the fragrance
of wayside roses increasingly ardent

as the younger man races ahead of the older,
the boy with fiery eyes
he first spied through a narrow window,
his face shining

onto the marketplace like Leto's son,
pouring sunlight on them,
happiness
and shadowless passion

and so pursued despite his more youthful wingèd feet
to make love to
beneath almond trees
fast shedding their petals.

A Beachside Memorial

Wiry sticks bind five logs forty
feet long, two wide,
sooty, sea-slimy.
Driftwood is tied
to salvaged ship planks.
Plowed sandbanks
are used as ballast. Whitecaps,
pink, gold, amber, slap
against the work, undermined
by rising currents. His friends pour gasoline
on it, together help set
it on fire, watch the flames soar,
crackling, popping, sweat
from the sea seeping out its water-logged pores.

Before the wind returns, the salty air stinks
of death, disemboweled crab,
gnawed fish heads.
The ocean is a flat, slab-
gray sea reeling like a drunkard drinking
the last of sunset, a wine
it's always thirsty for.

                    The fog looms like a shroud
over the horizon as the crowd
warms itself by the bonfire's embers.
It is a cold night, even colder at water's
edge. The coals sizzle, spit, steam
as waves wash over them like creatures lured
in by the scent of the logs' ashes they seem
to hunger for, as if they were those of the boy they'd drowned.

Haydn

To every thing there is a season
and all are of dust and to dust
return, for who shall bring anyone
to see or hear of what in time must

follow him? An old man lies awake
at night brooding on the fate
that awaits him, not able to fake
it or pretend again that sure date

with destiny has not already been
determined. And yet what obsesses
him more are his final seconds when
he'll know for certain his fixed brief lease

on life is over, cancelled forever.
At that perilous moment, what will he hear,
what will he see or imagine? His lover
standing near him to quell his fear

of oblivion? All his life, he has prayed
to be spared the dangers a man
faces in his dying vision, to be saved
from the demons inside him by Haydn,

say, one of his quartets, the Lark,
maybe, or the Sunrise played,
as if someone long ago in the dark
of night is embracing him, like a serenade

letting him know, assuring him that he has been
happy more than once in his life,
that despite his sinful pride, he'd seen
much kindness, beauty, felt a love surviving the strife

and fears and terrors and pain of living in a tragic
world. That is what he prays for, the sense
of being alive revealed in a few bars of music,
the last notes he'll hear before all he cherishes dies into silence.

Resurrection

At night's end, in a starless sky, a dusky moon,
looming over trees, rests in a thin silver, blue-
tinted crescent as first light brightens shadows
below the hills, the dark moon darkening to
an abyss, a black hole that might soon
swallow the world while he dreams. No man knows
anything of such things. Of indeterminate
age, lying by a river, I watch as it flows
always changing, the hour never too late,
while I pray for peace, patience, and penitence
though I am far from cities, people, pestilence,
with little time left for me to lose or to gain,
wondering how I might end or if it might happen again,
like a rising back into life with the sun in the morning, eager, insatiate.

Moonlight in Childhood

1.

Winter thrills the air, the faraway thunder
of storm clouds, a bleak season,
fearful in its way, but deserving wonder,
too, defying sense, betraying reason,

the moon gleaming on snow packs
recently piled on gardens, walkways,
forest floors, though foxes' bones, racks
of stags' antlers, snakes' skins, a maze

of feathers, eggs shells, birds' nests
fallen last spring from limbs, branches
lie sheltered now where each rests
in cold comfort beyond where moonlight reaches,

moonlight white like snow on which shadows
are slowly walking across
a field glistering white. Who knows,
if you don't, where they're going, as if some loss

has made them forget their way back under a black
but luminous sky? The boy stares out, trying
to see better, hoping to track
or trace all the known constellations, if nothing

else guides him, but the stars are frozen in place,
lightless, stupefied by the sight
of men, hunters maybe, after the chase
desperately lost, too hapless to know what is right.

Oh, moon, companion of his childhood,
though, like you, he might fade
away at dawn, how loving, good,
kind you've been to him, his shade

drawn open so he might watch you shine
through windows. They have lasted
a lifetime, its specters like a sign
he drew on his ceiling each night, flickering, blurred
as the men he once spied hiking upon a snow-
laden field past midnight, longing
for home and warmth, he supposed,
cold as winter moonlight, transient and darkly glowing.

2.

Moonlight in shadows
the clarities
of darkness,

what it bestows,
what it sees
not less

but more than what day
illuminates,
keen

to shine too brightly. The play,
as it hesitates,
between what is seen

and opacity: the spiny edges
of leaves, trees'
strict trunks, an owl

in flight, a wall of hedges
abutting a field, bees'
hives, fowl-

feathered-delicate and papery,
hidden deep
in woods so subdued by night

it is easy
to lose one's way as in a sleep
morning light might

fail to awaken you. The earth stirs with nocturnal
things the moon seems
to seek,

to point to, to call
to so that, as in dreams
or music,

unspoken images emerge
out of obscurity
as if born from within it

are profounder languages
than a child has the capacity
to hear or to understand unless he, too, is moonlit.

.

Every Beach Is a Cemetery

1.

Over these waters, destroyers, battle ships,
carriers sailed to the war. Near the dunes
bulwarks kept watch. Beach grass whips
in the wind among sea oats. Ice plant blooms

in patches like scraggly rugs thrown down
among wiry nettles a cottony fiber
sticks to. Yellow green moss clings to brown
and ash-colored sand where storms and high water

yesterday revealed the bony, buried wreck
of the Prince Philip, the timber of its rotted
hull like whale's ribs picked clean, entombed
on this beach after it sank in eighteen eighty six

during a Shakespearean tempest, its crew lost.
This morning, the moon is the Halloween
orange of streetlights in fog. Gulls, tossed
by wind-gusts, cry for their dead the way humans keen.

2.

A fin whale's carcass lies at tide's edge, black skin
bitten white, its blubber gray, runny,
viscous as wet cement. It stinks, every fin
decaying, oozing on the beach which the sea,
retreating, cannot wash clean for hours
or days. A dozer is digging a grave at the foot
of a dune. Slowly, carefully as a crowd cowers
before it, it shoves the whale into the boot-
shaped pit, packs, then smoothes the sand firm
so no one will be able to guess a buried whale
lies beneath. Now rare in these waters, it thrills

the spirit to see one swimming. But it came to harm,
this one, prey to man or beast or disease, the pale,
glassy bright cast of its bulging eyes like Melville's
white sperm whale's perhaps, imploring, Why did life fail me?

    3.

Bewhiskered seals lying on a Cliff House rock,
sand dollars, a surfer on his board floating
alone, a boulder the sea has sculpted to a block

of pocked cement, a glass jar bobbing, waiting
for waves to toss it on the beach, driftwood,
chipped shells, dried seaweed, a marble-white,

red-and-silver-veined stone, a soft gray hood
of fog hiding Sutro Heights on an autumn night:
tracks and traces of things as they are, the great,

good place of the world tremulous with a light,
intensified by sunset, squawking crows fly through.
Shadows cast by wind-blown, scraggly Monterey pine

dangle over rock face. The sea's power is never satiated,
terror gleaming round it as if from Leviathan's teeth,
its eyes like the eyelids of dawn, like torches more fiery

than sunset flashing out of its mouth: the awe it bequeaths
the meaning, source, and origin of all liturgy,
every beach littered with lost lives, every beach a cemetery.

    4.

Things as they are. Groggy seals, otters, a surfer alone,
a jam jar tossed intact on the beach, driftwood,
a soaked scarlet scarf, a polished, iridescent stone:
random things, each in its own way sufficient, each good.

But the wind is changing. A few close shutters against
the cold to come. Far off, crab boats resemble small islands.
The sea remains calm, though pelicans have sensed
shifting weather, flying as a flock over drifting sands.

A lone man walks in the park past vines and brush, a pathless
thicket dense as a forest's. Migratory birds
rest by a lake that raccoons slip in through a mess
of dense ferns and algae as the sun, refuting useless words,

descends lower over the horizon, below clouds, a radiant
sunset widening the sky, filling the blessed country
of night with a final light that has nothing to recant
or regret since all it leaves behind is accomplished by necessity.

III

Winter Solstice

Feeling bored, he walks along a rocky
shoreline, past piers and a long
abandoned harbor, nothing to see
that interests him. It is not wrong
on a day this short to yield to ennui.
No ships depart from ice-bound
harbors, no cars are driven
on slick roadways. To feel sad
on the shortest day is no sin.
Despair turns hearts hard as stone.
At twilight he walks toward
the headlands' chalk cliffs, bone-
bare, to pick up a rock like a shard
he pockets to save a precious memory.

What time might spare or abandon, who
can say now? The ocean along the coast
is icy, the white water whiter than snow.
What would it tell you if I could show you
what I feel inside me? I suppose lost,
you might say. It is hard for you to know,
staring down at me from the seawall
though you might guess where I'd prefer
to be this bleak, frigid evening: the call
of ancient places I've dreamt of summoning us back,
the ice-bound coastline spied from a long boat, the fir-
lined coasts Vikings ravaged, naked Goths preparing to attack
the Romans. That is what I would see, my love, the year's longest
night. You and I like warriors in the Nordic dark, fearless in the forest.

Two white tailed kites fly past in tight alignment with the darkening
horizon, wings rippling like ribbons to crests in the air.
Crackling under foot, frost encrusted weeds cling
in patches to the slippery path. An icy sun burns through bare
clouds, the sky a brief glacier blue. I feel a cold exaltation

as we shiver in the salt-scented breezes. The last light shimmers
on a rain wet trail and trees as the heavens open one
last time to a sun slipping beneath hills of redwoods, firs,
madrones, bay laurels, live oaks whose bold, stark
outlines blacken the shadows they cast toward the east,
inscrutable as the pitch dark crevices in the cliff walls. And so we stroll,
or loll, never breaking our silence, neither of us with an enlightened remark
to make about life amidst such obscurity. When life is over, love has ceased
for us, let us speak of this, the world's longest night, as its chillingly somber soul.

It is Saint Lucy's Day, a rite to celebrate new light. I remember,
when I was young, ten girls even younger dressed in red
sashes, white dresses, wreathes worn in their plaited
hair decorated with wax candles whose flames would flicker
in our church's solemn darkness during their processional
toward the altar, the alms given, the greetings offered after in the hall
where cakes and buns were arrayed for the feast during brutal weather.
There is a life long power to its mystery, to the ghosts the candles cast
on our church's arched ceiling, its majestic high walls,
and night-darkened stained glass windows, their shadows leaping
and jumping, looming, almost trembling as the girls passed
by our pews and gathered round Pastor Fischer, the choir singing
all the while the old Lutheran hymns. What lures me back there, what calls
me now? Candle light and shadows in the sanctuary. The tenebrous glow of believing.

.

Christmas Morning

A bleak morning, winter-dark. Moon-lit waves
crash like an avalanche. On the hump of a dune,
a surfer, quiet, imposing as a statue hewn
from a tree trunk, contemplates
currents, how the riptides break.
Wave upon wave smashes on shore, swelling
dangerously high. Does he feel an ache
rising inside him as he watches the sea-surge with nothing
to do but wait? It is Christmas morning. Whiter
and whiter, the waves plunge, pound into
each other. Smoky rain clouds loom closer.
Ignited by sunrise, a fiery light, like a clue
to whatever the surfer is searching for, glistens,
gleams off the feathers of gulls and plovers as they take
off as one from the beach, wind-borne somewhere for no known reasons.

A nativity scene in a front yard. A swaddled baby,
an old, bent father, a young mother blest
by angels, shepherds, a star, three magi
carved from wood and displayed as best
they can be on a windy, unlit corner. It is early
morning still and snowing where you live, far too
cold and icy for me to fly home. For a moment,
I hear a past Christmas Eve mass being said
as we strolled in soft snow, recalling the scent
of incense, wax candles, the green and red
of poinsettia by the altar. Was any of it true?
Next morning, outside your window, a cherry tree,
in the midst of bare winter, perfumed the air, fragrant
as spring while it appeared to blossom from the sudden
burst of sunshine upon its ice-covered branches as if it were no illusion.

An amber full moon is slowly sinking in a Prussian blue sky,
dotted with stars. It is shortly before first light. A jet
flies westward. The king tide will reach its highest
soon. The sky will grow pale after the moon has set.

Near the horizon, clouds billow like sails unfurling
to a shifting wind. No one is walking the beach this early,
just me and my dog. The highway is quiet. A ring
of gray gulls dozes by a dune. Crows perch woodenly
like carvings from driftwood on the seawall. Streetlights flash
red green, green red, the sole Christmas colors in view.
The ocean turns a deep marine satin sheen, Arctic blue,
its breakers glacier white as the sun, in its first splash
of light, rises into sight on a morning that feels new born
as it climbs brighter over the hills and well above the sleepy city
awakened by its brilliancy, its glare intense, fixed as the eyes of an icon.

The Morning of the Last Day of the Year

In the grimy early morning dark of New Year's Eve
day, I dreamed of someone I'd known summoning me
from faraway where two men were unable to leave
or escape a fishing boat, trapped by fire. I could see
the flames charring their bodies into silhouettes.
Startled by the horror I woke, sensing their pain,
my heart racing, my body on fire, the incessant
swooshing sound of tinnitus freely pounding again
in my ears, its pulsing beat unceasing even after
a phantom friend from as faraway as the dreadful scene
I'd dreamed of cried to me to say what the disaster
might have meant. "Each man is responsible for his own
damnation," he warned, his voice hollowed by age, lean,
weakened by death. "Your pride has brought you down,
my friend. Your need to win. To beat the sea. Your failure to love."

Dreams are sometimes true, my dearest. To love as the dove
of the spirit (you'll know what I mean) loves the earth,
all that inhabits the world, the good, common, simple
ways we delight in being alive: it wasn't enough. I'm worth
more than that, I used to think. Yet now I'm a feeble
old man, in scary ways similar to the elderly Faustus
at the start of Marlowe's play (how it haunts me) whose will,
whose quest for knowledge, whose carnal lust, lust
for power were what creativity meant, the ill,
the weak, the ignorant, the submissive too deficient in passion
to matter. Myself am hell. It's so. Ah, Mephisto. Comprehension
comes too late, like an honest confession. I regret all
the good I have failed to do, unable to give myself selflessly. The Fall
from any paradise is, perhaps, the just punishment awarded
those who confuse love with pride, whose vanity defies the intransigent dead.

Today's is a rainy New Year's Eve morning. The drought might be over
soon. The Great Highway is flooded, the city magically
transported, apparitional, from the constant hard shower
pouring upon it, a vast scrim lit by streetlights. Except for the sea,
roaring loud as enraged krakens, it's quiet, the water, near dawn,
racing through streets mottled, sod green, brown,
thick with run-off, waste, cast off things. I hear you yawn
under the comforter, not quite sleeping, then softly snoring. Down
the bed, by your thighs, our dog is lying beside you for warmth.
Despite the light shining through a slit in our heavy curtains,
even to my restless, over alert eyes our house inside is so dark
I trust you can't see me pacing while waiting for the rains
to stop. It feels a bit like I'm praying to God on this year's last, stark
morning. To abiding love, I mean: old worlds seen anew, lost lives forgiving
me, forgotten joys spoken of again, the unknown dreams to come: kind, surprising.

The Morning of the First Day of the Year

Last night, only a few stars shone round
the gibbous moon in a flat matte black
sky. Hours before twelve, the raucous sound
of bombs going off began, like an attack
out of the sea by an enemy, fountains,
too, spiraling rockets, fireworks. This morning,
on The Great Highway, debris from the explosions
lie in little piles, red frayed paper, burning
residue of embers, boxes with red-tongued demons
imprinted on them used to shoot bombs
like guns randomly toward earth and heaven,
the louder the noise the more fear they'd create.
The remains of a few bonfires, like ashes scattered on tombs,
smolder on dunes. Seaside, arm in arm, two lovers wait
for the sun as if seeking from daylight some soon to come safe haven.

Before dawn, wearing hip-high waders, denim
work slacks held up by suspenders, thick
water-proof jackets, six crabbers, in the dim
glow of the moon, walk out zig-zag, quick
in their movements, into the tide, their flash
lights hunting for crabs flushed closer to the shore
by yesterday's big storms. They're aware it's rash
of them to leave the beach's safety, the sea more
dangerous at low tide when the waves appear
to have crested, flowing gently, like water
in a creek, and savvy enough of the risks to fear
the sudden sidewise slap of a rogue wave higher
than they are tall tossing them over into currents
that could carry them away from the spray and splash
of waves into a sea that, though it knows nothing, knows no accidents.

First light: yet this is still no place to seek silence
from, waves cracking like ice floes breaking,
the winds' power perpetuating the violence
of yesterday's outbursts. While the seawall's being
breached, whitecaps rise and crash on
the ocean as far away as the Farallons, the sun
low yet bulbous and ruddy. Ravens scurry in ritual
circles, mimicking a dirge above the pounding
of the waves. The wide beach, so crowded, full
of revelers last night, is empty. Leeward, a gull
shrieks back at the cries of the sea-surge. Even the crabbers,
braving the waves for the feast to come, to a man
have all left for home. Listen. It is the first day of a new
year. Say time instead has been suspended, is in abeyance. What can
you make, then, of this scene if changeless? Of the future, what does it tell you?

Waves break apart, collapse while fighting each other,
riptides clash. It is almost noon. A plover
flock picks at a bed of kelp. I went away
for a while. When I came back, the sea
for a moment seemed to open to the new day
the way sunflowers unfurl to the sun, to plea
to it for more light, ever more, even after
the clouds' vanishing had filled the world with
fresh radiance. The waves as they break and break
might be letting us know better about time,
how it repeats itself out of necessity, for the sake
of the music inherent in things. I gaze at the always shifting,
threatened shoreline. Can two unlike lives ever rhyme?
I could not survive without you, my love. The sea is no myth
but a glimpse of reality. All that it takes from us, all that it promises to bring.

Green

No more to wake to winter's brown fields and bleakly naked trees
now the dogwood, crocus, jessamine have bud
and bloomed. Migratory birds, ducks, geese
a few heron return. The sludge, muck, mud
of mid-March springs to life, grass, moss,
leaves shimmeringly green under a May sun.
A fox's fur gleams a golden red, with a gloss
to it like roosters' feathers or combs. One
black snake twists round another on a warm
flat black rock by the river. Near a patch of lady's
slippers and a thicket of wild roses, a swarm
of bees buzzes round their petals while a breeze's
heat enhances the bright verdant leaves of shaded jacks-
in-the-pulpit. The good world, it's said, consists of facts
like these that mean to free every last thought from harm.

If one trusts that the moss on tree trunks will turn velvet green
soon, the grasses green as mint, the air pungently
green, sharper than pine resin, then everything seen
by dawn shall shine a first-light-green. Mice that scurry
across a split log into a fireweed thicket will do so,
dew on wild grape flowers, or bent ferns, too, thirstily
drinking from pools night has dripped onto stones.
Shivering willows, their thin limbs and stems, as if new
to the world, will lazily shake themselves awake,
and meadows will glimmer the pale yellow-green of the apple
you carry that, when you bite into it, releases a sweetly
sour flavor that tastes of last fall's dying colors,
smells of its ember-like odors, senses you're meant to savor, to take
deeper thought in later, as if there is in the birth of a new green world the will
to return to, to recapture autumn's last flourish of beauty and all the lives it owns.

Blue-Green

The white-capped, aspiring, wild, over-lapping waves are
rambunctious, almost riotous this late morning,
the sea the somber blue-green, seen from afar,
of spruce woods in winter, of magnolia leaves in spring,
of ponds or bogs grown algae-dark in summer,
of northern skies in late autumn before the first snow
begins to fall, twilight subdued, made dimmer
by storm clouds reflecting the pine forests below
as they crash like waves rolling through the sky.
It is the luxurious blue-green of the sleeves on the blouse
of one of Bronzino's loveliest boys, the sole surviving eye,
jewel-cruel and hard, on the lid of an Egyptian sarcophagus,
the plush velvet divan a lady lounges on in a Victorian
portrait. It is the color of truth, whatever the day or season,
when bright cloudless skies let glassy-blue seas widen and deepen and darken.

Three Colors of Desire

1.

The steel blue of loss. The royal blue
of sorrow, of my life without you.

The neon blue of grief, the blue of flood
lights scouring our neighborhood.

The della Robbia blue of mercy, the Virgin's
robes, the tears she sheds for our sins.

The blue of heartbreak, blue as Chinese porcelain,
of your birthstone, of not ever seeing you again.

Missing you the icy blue of Nordic rivers,
fed by fjords. Of rafting their risky waters.

The blue of regrets, of the flawed aquamarine
goblet you bought, your faux Ming screen.

The blue of the sea wall where I met you,
the blue of unhealed bruises, old or new,

the true blue of lovers, the lavender
blue of a field of asters, the blue of disaster,

the flecked, turquoise blue of your eyes,
your torn boxer shorts, your fibs and lies,

the wailed jazzy blue of dawn shining
on our rumpled bed, the blue of my grieving,

the blue of desire, the blue of two lovers
recklessly pursuing the joys of a summer's

sky that was the azure blue of Debussy's
aquarelle music or Hiroshige's more turbulent seas

the blue of the sky we last lay under and made love to,
two blue flames burning out to ash the blue night you

left me. The blue of the ecstasy of new passion after,
like your faraway music, its oceanic laughter.

2.

Your betrayal is white as a bathroom mirror is, fostered by
falsity, fogged by your breath, like the white lie

you told by divorcing me. White as your wedding dress
flowing freely, wind-blown by your need to confess

you detested me. White as the note you wrote
saying I had sinned against you, a letter I could quote

from memory years later. The white of your face,
meticulously powdered to leave no trace

of his kisses. The white of my desire unconsummated,
of sheets I'd left unstained, of a bed

we uneasily slept in, of no seed spilled on your underwear,
of your ivory-white teeth exposed as you'd dare

me to screw you after him. The white of an avalanche smashing
down on Chamonix, the impotent revanchist raging

inside me, a longing for revenge unsatisfied
by anger alone, the white pus I oozed from the unhealed

wound of your infidelity. Look how the rain is falling whiter than
yesterday's snow, whiter than sorrow before it began,

I mean the mourning that is my impotence, the silence
that lies to you in my passion's abeyance.

You've shed a tear, single pearl-white tear, insincere
as a child's, down your cheek, white as fear,

white as owl's feathers, bats' teeth, tree fungus
toad stools, limestone, white as us

against the backdrop of a night-dark, forest-
like cell we can find no rest

in, you inside, me outside, a study in contrast,
a separation that cannot last

till morning. On the finger where you had worn your wedding
ring, there's a band of flesh fading

into the white of peeling skin, of the voice, before it has broken,
of a choir boy, sexless, angelic, blameless, unfallen.

3.

The unjustified, stunning red of dying things: stars, embers,
cheeks struck by a hectic, by love's mounting fevers.

Look where you will. Red is never impartial or fair.
Lipsticks. Wall-sized posters. Cars, trucks. Ruby hair.

Theater cushions. Slot machine's cherries. Warning lights
on cop cars or ambulances. Red is whatever ignites

a night on fire, bright as the bleeding crimson of bruises
or wounds. Is whatever evidence accuses

you of, though you're innocent as a book's
unthumbed ruddy bindings, the black words inside it. How a priest looks

at you as you pass by him on your thoughtless way
will ruin your day, like a judge who refuses to say

what you are guilty of while you blush with the passion
you wish to hide from him, weighing on

you as it does. Say innocence is the red of Christ's blood
that colors the wine while improving its flavor, too good

to swallow all in one gulp. Or the red cross
on the flag that rescues you when loss

is imminent. Yes, your lover has slept with another.
At love you are such a beginner

it is no wonder you mistake it for judgement,
as anyone innocent

as you might do. Study the red of the thread
in a tapestry, how each stitch has led

the saint depicted in it to his martyrdom, his judges
more obsessed with their duplicities

than with his righteousness. Red, then, as the Buddha's Fire
Sermon, lest compassion be undone by desire.

See? A black-spotted tokay lizard killed
by a red-furred cat it was made to fight

is smothered by ants whose feelers are alert,
hungry for gecko, appetite-willed

by a need to survive, as night
devours day, not to hurt

the creature further since the lizard's life is done
for already, finished, each insect red as flames

smoldering, burning:
not desire vanishing

like smoke from a pyre by the holy river,
but the fear

its wild crackling has kindled in your ears,
words you cannot hear

as your lover prays to be freed of his pain no one blames
you for, my dear, while chanting your sanguine thousand sacred names.

Two Riddles of Translation

1.

The screen is much too wide to absorb it all in in one view.
Yet if one stands far back enough, the mountains (like
gigantic moss-covered pine cones, lean, bent askew
by time and wind) reveal slopes too sheer to hike.
The wars are happening elsewhere, if unseen, untrue.
Move from panel to panel. Much is depicted in miniature,
minuscule cranes, two men poling two tiny boats
on a river widening as it flows from the east. Culture
is history stilled, it says. Never able to move, a duck floats
in place downstream. High up, in a wood hut, two men,
in fluent robes, converse while gesturing, their agèd faces
little more than a few quick brush strokes. In a den
of sorts, not quite the mouth of a cave, a solitary monk
sits praying. Or, shaded by clouds, is he thinking of a plum tree trunk?

2.

The dawn this morning is a rosy Greek dawn, eos
rhododáktylos, and the sea, thálassa, is a Greek
sea, dark as grape pulp or the dregs in a wine
cup. In a cove, north, off the Marin coast,
I spy ships, ram-headed, dolphin-eyed,
waiting for hints of a breeze, the freed winds
that will carry men to Troy. Over the Farallons–
hidden in mist, ghostly, ragged as Skylla's
teeth–gulls fly sunward in circles, their cry
like Ariadne's, abandoned, love-sick. It is still night
in the shadows of dunes, darker in the cave I am standing by
to greet the famous Ancient who said, "Poetry is not wisdom
since the dead live silenced by eternal sorrow." Yet, if I pour
him blood to quench his thirst, will he tell me his name again, repeat his tragic story?

IV

A Fable

A frightened bird—a light feathery orange, a bolder downy red—
sings as if to comfort a boy trying to play on a schoolyard
swing while crying, his brother in a sand box dreaming of bed
as their sister worries, rocking on a teeter-totter. Regard
them well, these children in my fable whose father lets them stay until
it is twilight, though he knows what awaits them all before their darkened doorsill.

So let us imagine they listen to the frightened bird's song. A beautiful bird
bejeweled like a red sapphire in a chalice ringed by amber
in this parable of a romantic sort I have devised so it be heard
gently, quietly, before the world is betrayed into silence by all but their savior,
the bird, who, beyond human greed and pride and ken, long ago, even then,
by a war's blasted woods sang its song of solace in despite of twilight, in despair of
men.

A Ladder

The fog-drenched cliffs are slippery, hard, tricky to climb
up from the beach, ninety feet or more,
fearful of losing footing. It's a long time
since I've watched sunrise here. Far from shore,
a liner heads west. The beach is windy
in the mist. I'm a child again, counting each rung
of the ladder I'd been forbidden to climb by my
father onto the roof of our garage to look. I was young
when I fell, slipping off wet shingles onto the ground thirty
feet below. I'd been blinded by the sun as it broke
through the pine while I stood on the roof staring directly
at it, into it, daring it. I lay on my father's groomed lawn,
not quite unconscious, struggling to breathe, stunned. No one spoke.
Immensity had claimed me. Undone me. The fearsome glory of naked dawn.

Brahms, Op. 116

A late November early evening quiet, breathless as it waits for sunset.
The trees across the hills slope down toward a winding, shallow
valley. Birches, chestnuts, cypress, fir weave a densely threaded net
against the sky: gnarly vines, tangled ivy, mossy loam, spindly ferns below.

Lars watches from his window, the sun already invisible behind a thicket
of leafless limbs and spiky needles. As he listens to the music after
he's stopping playing it, as its sad beauty lingers inside him, why can't he forget
for a moment he's dying? Dusk outside briefly brightens, then grows dimmer:

first dark orange, then a blood red that seeps into scarlet, a somber, fiery maroon.
Darkness fast follows, falling silent like the music he's recalling when, suddenly,
something in the opening melodic line of the G major sextet is like the moon
outside, shining in the dark with a formal light, cathartic as Brahms' lovely melancholy.

Which is his music's glory, too. How it is always about night, the coming of night,
night after night, the beautiful way day has of dying time after time in late fall.
What will music sound like as his soul wanders far away, passing into a last twilight?
On a hospital upright, he plays Op. 116, its music grave, patient, stoically inconsolable.

Son

Son, my unborn son lying in my arms,
awake, crying, son of no wife,
eyes open as if fearful of the life
to come, the vanishing sun that alarms
him like a dream that itself
is dying in the dusk. A breeze whispers
through a window rumors
of spring. I'd tell him of the shelf
of books I've saved to read him
someday, but night as it falls speaks
with more authority. I embrace
him tighter. It is cold outside.   By dim,
shimmering stars, his cat-keen eyes chase
after the moon until he spies it where it rises and breaks
into slivers like late winter ice in the river that floods by our farm
where I keep him safe from harm, my son.

Compassion

1.

The moon's a pale
ball above
a tree-lined horizon

rising full sail
out of
a dragon

green canopy.
Sunset
glows rose red, a rainbow's

misty yellow. Anachronistically
meaningful, the duet
between them shows

you how to read the trees'
calligraphy
brushed the ancient ways

with a hand that frees
the eye to see
why night's clarity is keener than day's.

2.

In the park,
October
burns the leaves

and grass dark
as amber-
colored sap or bronze bark, deceives

your eyes with
its brightness,
sunlight flaky as rust.

For the fifth
day, the press
of ash and dust

on the air makes it hard
to breathe,
the body

oppressed by its disregard
for what seethes
through the intensity

of it,
a veracity
nearly unbearable

when the way before you is lit
not for you to see
but for it to be invisible.

3.

Truth's first story
is often lost
to history, myth,

fantasy–
like a ghost
haunting me daily with

its tricks as I walk beside it,
like mythology
strutting behind me,

Why won't I admit
'mystery'
means only that I cannot see

it if it's a story, legend, fable
I'm unable
to understand

directly, incapable
of the faith of an Abel,
that the hand

of God in creation is not knowledge
but perceptions,
intimations,

a pledge
that beyond the visible horizons
lie other lands and skies and oceans?

4.

And thus, irredeemable, beyond the
historically visible,
Achilles

mourns by the sea
unable
to fight, his sword, greaves

waiting by his side
he as good as dead
as prophesied, no

immortal like the one who died
as was said,
crucified, with a promise to

come again,
glorified,
where, in each story

both so plain
even simplified
as they might be,

easy to mock,
portentous
nothings, nonsense, why do

I take stock,
momentous
reckonings of both, say each is true,

or at least does not lie,
however unfair
it is to tragedy,

to reality, the unsaid why
of suffering
all people feel, to suggest how today,

most strangely,
despite the sting
of time, ancient poems might show the way?

Achilles stands need deep
in the sea,
ponders his shadow black

as Thetis's waves while Jesus, unable to sleep,
eternally wades in the Galilee
up to his knees and never looks back.

    5.

My walk back
from the park is wet, muggy,
the doubt that returns

inside me, void, lack,
loss, the acuity
that comes from pain one learns

of merely from looking,
unafraid, at reality,
though it may be

too visible, everything
so simply
what it is, the sea,

the sun blank
white at noon,
its light still piercingly hot,

the rot, rank,
of raccoon
and rat, yet nothing not

unsure, the path
underfoot,
the canopy, the birds

or the wrath
to come, route
and way, Jesus last words

about death, emptiness,
what Achilles
saw too, forsakenness,

and Jesus's plea,
sabachthani,
the forgiving blessing

that silence can be,
the absolute's
muted Yes

heard, too, when Priam falls to his knees
begging to take his son's
body back

to his family so that the brutality, cruelty
violence of tragedy's
history might end, some day, in compassion.

Sutro Heights

Stand on the highest point of Sutro
Heights, near the ruins of a parapet,
beach and Great Highway far below,
waves dotted with evening surfers. Sunset
will arrive soon as the fog drifts in,
clouding the Pacific. The horizon
late in December is a thin
line of gray with the clarity of polished stone.
Sparrows sweep through wind-bent pines,
chirping noisily. The steep cliff
drops two hundred feet. The world is full of signs
or ciphers like an ancient hieroglyph's,
illegible, inscrutable as the mist slowly obscuring the city,
darkening the sea. This is not a story about estrangement,
but the beauty of winters by the Bay, the strangeness
of its exactitude, its clarities, precision, senseless
splendors. This morning after days of rain,
the storm's winds died just as the sun rose
and spilled over the highest hills,
though a few wispy, straying clouds still
shadowed the city. Flat as a Colorado plain,
the slate-gray ocean grew rippled by waves. Cattails, reeds
along the shoreline glistened in the murky water
flowing off the highway where rivulets and creeks
had formed from the runoff that cluttered gutters.
And the storm-darkened sea shone from its crests the amber
of cat's eyes as the ivy-entangled rock face of the Heights
turned into the wall of a temple, quartz yellow and gold and crystalline whites.

The Pond

Do a man's imaginings annihilate reality, darken everything,
even the sun's stark glare on material matters? New green
plants, if lucky, display their loveliest foliage in the spring
until invasive weeds, like kudzu, subdue them, obscene
in their easy profligacy. How wantonly, thickly it grows
dominant except where the canopy's deep shadows
deny it sun. Here a skin of moss, in a creek-dug ditch,
clings to bones and tree bark as to stones in a cemetery.
In a pond edged with reeds, stumps black as pitch
lurk out of the shallows like creatures who'd prefer opacity
to light, the pool's swampy surface infested with scum
and algae, its muddy banks cluttered with queen annes lace,
mayweed, scattered briars, last fall's breezes rotted leaves.
What are you looking for, what is the fear that seems to seize
you, what anxiety, when a forest summons you to share its freedom?

And so you've hiked further in. Why not let woods shade you from
too much sun when reality is so glaringly bright it's dumb-
founding? When you reach the spot, you stare at skaters
gliding over a pond's filmy, frothy surface, watching
them feed on tiny insects while they dart on the water
this way and that, relentlessly, chaotically zigzagging
while, almost invisible, a backswimmer is floating,
hunting alone, its nature solitary like many spider's.
It prefers to eat immature mosquitoes. And that's good
and useful to humans. But only life's hunger for food
matters to nature. They'll eat almost anything, even including,
like cannibals, their own kind. Since by the end of spring
few young mosquitoes are left to be consumed, a backswimmer
threatened by starvation will eat whatever it can until it's the last hunter,
like imagination, patiently stalking prey in a drying green pond late into summer.

A Church

Everything on a hot day looks white. The trees, bushes,
grass are white. The orange tile and red
bricks and brown walls are white. I gaze
up at the sky, not blue or gray anymore but bled

of color, stainless. I recall a church I walked into
once to flee from a city's voices. The afternoon
chill of an icy-white sun pierced through
its rippled milk-white windows as if immune

from the taint of specificity, its ceiling pellucid as a sheet,
plain walls stripped of their cerise and rose
coats of paint, bare plaster gleaming like sleet
that, having fallen during the night, by sunrise glows

so brightly, luminously the whole vast earth appears
to flare white flames, pure and blinding the way
the Absolute is reputed to intensify all the years
of a life into the splendor of everything, with nothing more to say.

I watched the naked silver cross on the white altar
cloth burn away as if melting until a cloud
covered the sun outside like a shroud, like a blur
on a page that keeps you from knowing more than is allowed.

So I left the church and walked to the harbor, the horizon
ahead a dying silvery blue-gray, the buildings behind me
a defiant brazen copper and bronze while the setting sun
dyed sky and sea into a confusion of colors, pink and rust and ruddy.

Other Voices

A Letter from a Retired Professor to a Former Student

It's July 4th. My family liked awfully the fine sketch
you made of me and passed it around themselves
until I finally got it back. Families can be a wretch
sometimes. I miss you exceedingly. My bookshelves
are now organized, thanks to you. I'm having tea
with John in my backyard garden. My horse's recovered
from his bad near foreleg.   You know how I worry.
Life is so untrustworthy. But now he has at last mended.
Never lend your horse or your wife to your best friend.
An old stable joke. John startled a yearling yesterday
that leapt thirty feet across our great meadow, and Tom,
thank God, is off fishing for a week with the Todds. The end
of every semester is the hardest part. I look at the way
you have painted me with great pleasure. I miss you. Come
see me soon, have a great summer, may you find whatever you needed.

An Artist to a Younger Friend, Three Thousand Miles Away

I can't help but associate Shapero's music with those long-
ago days when his symphony became an anthem of some
sort for us. No work from me. Everything I make now feels wrong
somehow except for sketches on paper of a few gum
and maple trees half bare on the other side of the river.
Bob dislikes talking about art now and wants to hear only Mozart.
Winter and the virus have called attention to our ages, though
he stays abed later more, rueful that he's ninety two. My heart
beats erratically. Hemschemeyer visited and left a copy of her
weighty Akhmatova on the seat of our car with a note.   So kind
of her. We were able to sit on the deck and watch the river
and a pair of eagles diving for fish. I am able to write solely on lined
paper these days. Bob likes to talk, when he does, about his forays
into the Cedar Bar back in the fifties. It is a strange time in so many ways.
I hope we can survive it, though I detect the fading shadows of things wherever I
look.

An Anglican Priest to His Congregation on Pentecost

Appropriation happens whenever a former story or narrative
is divested of its original intention and reinvested in another.
Cinderella, say. Suppose she is not as naive or sensitive
as she's been depicted. When the prince tries the slipper
on her foot, she thinks to herself that he is not as handsome
as he was at the ball and has a long nose and bad breath.
So she scrunches up her foot so the slipper will not fit it.
But John's attempts to understand the life and death
of Jesus form from the Torah a free commentary which is lit
by the past it refuses to reject. Exodus' quail and manna come
to mean what Jesus says he is, the bread of heaven, each crumb
of it devoured along the trek of the Hebrew's desert years. The bread of life
nourishes our spirits forever. To cite that painful journey isn't the bad breath
that disillusions a wise Cinderella from becoming a wife. There's no strife
between the testaments' stories. It's how they pray per omnia saecula saeculorum.

A Ballet Critic on a Choreographer's "Beethoven Quartets"

It is here that his "Beethoven Quartets" particularly interest me.
Certainly it is an abstract ballet, but in another sense
it is not, as the Beethoven music itself, despite what you see
on the stage, is and is not. It is about something, this dance,
to which its entrechats and arabesques are ancillary,
meanings that the Mediterranean world perceives in the body,
the nude body which is what ballet is as it struggles to find
some way of expressing the ineffable matters essential
to the spirit of man, God, love, grief, death. How can the mind
of humanity be perfected by anything so silly, so trivial
as Gisele or Swan Lake or even Tristan and Isolde, the creaky
fustian of Lear or the preposterous in Dostoevski? Yet they do.
Like Christmas Eve, at least sometimes, they can magnify
the soul into believing in the joy of being in the world. And they can also
be about something so tenderly haunting I'd hesitate, for all our sakes, to name it here.

On Legibility

A moon-white chill hovers in the morning light diffused by
a gauzy fog looming over the city. San Francisco's
wet streets brighten boldly at sunrise. An eye
of a raven gazes at me from where it's perched in rows
of other birds on the wall of the promenade. The sea
is a solemn place at this transient hour, like a work
of art waiting to be unveiled. A sand dollar floats free
from a wave rippling high on the beach.. The water's murky
with driftwood churned up by storms. In a cove near the Cliff
House, a craggy boulder seems to be spying on me too,
watching me suspiciously. A dog barks at the waves. I am stiff
from old age. The mist chills my bones. The sun hovers behind me. Blue
anemones flower in the pools by caves as dawn's long shadows cast images
on rock face like petroglyphs by a forgotten people or indecipherable calligraphies.

Echo Park

Dozens of shirts are jumbled together in bins on a sidewalk.
Tank tops, I-shirts, V-necks, crew necks, and T-shirts,
their colors like the strips of purple, chartreuse, chalk
white, ruby crêpe paper that flap from the wood awning
of a shop. The afternoon sun is so hot it hurts
to think. Wisteria, bougainvillea, pink and red fuchsias
cling to iron trellises along stucco walls, dropping
their petals on the ground for passersby to walk
on as if they were on parade, worthy to cheer, to praise
for being alive. Old women poke through piles of shawls
as a girl opens a coral one as long as she is tall to gaze
at happily, wrapping it round her. Up the street, guys talk,
brag, smoke weed, their shiny shoes black, trousers, jeans
black and baggy, T-shirts sleeveless, white and tight. Each market's stalls
display goods bright as a cloudless sky that dazzles the eye with all that light means.

A Last Hike In

1.

Why do these woods, like words, matter, the wilderness
of my mind through which I wander still? What
do they signify? What remains of a life unless,
at the end, it is free to hike deeper in? It is a hot,

bright, vivid day. Thistles are growing out of red clay,
ivy-entwined thickets, dogwood, hidden in shade
and shadow until the sun's freed, cardinals, a jay,
a feral dog barking at noisy blue jays, a pale jade-

like green to the newest leaves and dew-wet grass,
rabbits racing over oaks' twisting, thick roots,
quick creeks leading to a widening lake. How to pass
another day here, swimming freely among minnows, newts,

two water snakes. And I, happy, as if new to the universe,
lying after on a muddy bank, a strong spring
storm on the way, raindrops weighty as pebbles, curse
myself for returning here, to this lake where the past is everything.

2.

Let memory be the wilderness I hide in to escape from time,
from worries and disappointments, to be spared the news
of more disasters lurking ahead. Believe me, I'm
aware my death pursues me there, too. I possess clues

left from my past to know how, in the near total dark
of the forest where as a boy fighting with vines,
struggling against ivy and brush, the oak and hickory bark
black as duff, fungus growing from stumps, I'd spy a few signs

of the extinct mammoth trees that once thrived there in air
always drizzling, the dew-heavy, thick canopy diffusing
light, dimming it to a dusk-like shimmering bronze, the scary
thick dark woods where I sought solace despite my forebodings.

Return home, old man, it says now. You needn't stay. Or go deeper
in, become more lost, if you must this late, than you
have trekked before. Silence. Absence. The fears that would deter
you. It is the wilderness inside you you're afraid of. The old made new.

3.

Is it too late for me to find a place to return to, to embrace,
to subdue my fears? to believe in the passion I
thought old age had denied me too soon, that trace
of the trail or path or way ahead, when young I'd failed, why

I do not know, to dare past its obvious dangers? Enticing woods.
Intimations of sycamore, poplar, oak, spruce, maple, hickory,
sweet gum, pine, of wind and sun and welcoming sky. My childhood's
woods should comfort me, hold me, that darkling time, that sapling tree,

now and forever. Trees unfurling leaves, morning skies the faded blue
and white of cornflowers, hydrangea, the air shimmering
as if to the sound of a river's murmurs and reverberations, the mind true
to what it conceives like late spring flowers rising or lost spirits budding

out of rain-softened ground. What is it a fading mind feels, hears, sees?
Is it a day ripe for a walk round a lake, a slow stroll to catch a glance
of a secret meadow, milkweed stalks, emerald days, lilies
by a creek, jays berating the heat, wild rose petals (in a gentle dance

the wind induces in them) drifting freely, spiraling down like feathers,
ferns and soft grass to lie on as I watch chips of pine bark floating
on a stream like tiny paper boats sailing far from my sight, the air thickening
from the damp earth, all the green world I never meant to leave, what gathers

now in my mind like a last image while a final evening descends upon me
shading hills, shadowing woods, blackening every tree until each
living thing is gathered up into the arms of night while, curiously, I see
a praying mantis devouring a milk white anise butterfly that, as if to beseech

heaven, flutters its wings for a while as slowly as a gliding, soaring bird, beautifully
lifted by breezes higher into the air than twilight's obscuring sky, beyond life's reach?

Tractatus

1.

The new moon the birds wake
to is slipping
from the sky,

the Pacific lake-
still, high tide nipping
at a beachside cliff as if to try

its patience as a cat
might tease a ball of twine
it is slowly unraveling.

Two late stars in a flat,
gray sky shine
dimly, yet everything

about them is beautiful,
though they're quick
to fade in the morning

sun, almost invisible
by dawn, each a wick
flickering

in a pool of candle wax,
the horizon
thin as silk threads,

pale as chalk marks or cracks
in a sidewalk, bone-
white. A pelican spreads

its wings out wide as the moon,
a scimitar-shaped
crescent

it might fly to, rest in soon,
guided
by its light to mimic its descent.

The sun surprises, its view
of the world raw,
fresh, new,

yet with nothing make-do
about it, like a law
of blue

sky nothing can disobey, the light
so bright it blinds our eyes, yours
and mine, as if its power,

its brilliance descends upon us to re-write
our world as it pours
forth its glory as it chooses, waiting for departure's hour.

2.

Maybe all of life is a struggle to illuminate the meaning
of just a few words. To make one thing clear. Bring
their senses out of hiding. A high tide is sweeping the beach
free of debris, the wide strand white as snow under
a blank sky as the fog-veiled dawn sun, bleach
white, hesitantly rises over the eastern hills. White water
is turbulent far as the Farallon Islands left invisible
by the mist that obscures all of the city, too. The dunes'
tall sea oats tremble in the cool, swift breezes. All is well.
Seals sleep peacefully on their rocks, like cartoons
of themselves, simple, fed, content, plump, and logy
until the sun burns off the fog with an aura of majesty,
commanding obedience, demanding, insisting we all look
at the world more attentively at last, in noon's intensified clarity,
each thing exactly what it is: tree, plover, house, runner, bench, book,
cars on the highway. So much we have to say of them. So much there's left to tell.

To My Husband

Dawn star, half moon travel together, not alone.
A winter wind whips the ocean. Sand
pricks our faces. I hear the groan
of someone sad not far away. I hold your hand.

We are both a little sea-drunk. Night
strong gusts pile dunes on the highway.
Where the earth curves back, a slight
bright line cracks open a way out. It is our day

to slip through time, space, not too late
for grace, the word we spoke to defy fate
like two men saved from shipwreck, star-
guided by love, if we say it, wading to safety near the harbor.

Notes to Other Voices

The professor is Robert Barnes Rudd, a professor emeritus of English at Hamilton College when I was there, an elderly man who continued to ride his horse late in his life, often appeared walking on campus wearing jodhpurs and carrying a riding stick, and was famous for giving parties for students in which everyone, while having a fine time of it keeping warm by the hearth, drank too much. Each year, at the college's Christmastide celebrations before the holiday break, he read Christmas poems, mostly from the Renaissance, to the teachers and students gathered in a hall designed like a Tudor great room, always ending with Eliot's Journey of the Magi. Despite his raspy, slightly phlegmy, very old man's voice, he read with such passion and intensity that it moved everyone, a few to tears. Who is like him on any campus in the world today? No one I suspect. It is right to say, for all his quirks and many improprieties in his latter years, and there were many, he was truly and memorably beloved.

The artist is Gerald Coble about whom I have written often in my work, my earliest and in some ways most important tutor, mentor, initiator into what it means to be an artist. He painted, sculpted, drew, made collages, listened to all the music he could, and read everything he thought he should read, including all of Proust several times over. He showed his art infrequently, but he never stopped working up until he died of heart failure at eighty nine. I was seventeen when we met; he was twenty seven. No one in my life was more important to me throughout my life for what he gave me when I was young. I still see much of the world through his eyes, through the landscapes I watched him painting during the year we were together and for sixty years thereafter.

The priest is George Tuma, a priest in the more or less Anglo-Catholic traditions of American Episcopalians, and a medievalist with a doctorate from the University of Michigan. At SF State, George and I shared an office for twenty years. His faith was always tottering, always on the edge of some abyss about which he did not speak, yet into which he never fell completely, I hope. He was one of the kindest, gentlest, most compassionate men I have ever known and behaved so with all his students as well, never faltering, never getting angry at or impatient or bored with anyone of them that I ever saw. He loved his daughters, his second wife, and his four large, long haired dachshunds with a love that radiated from him each time I saw him with them. He suffered so much with his second wife's pain during her long, long illness, I think it killed him at the end, too. He was the sort of man who would say No when he meant Yes at the beginning of a sentence in response to whatever it was I or anyone had said. I think his life might have been a bit like that. I mean the way he would speak of doubt as if it were faith.

The critic is Bob Stephens, one of my dearest friends for over fifty years. He introduced me to, among other poets, Jack Gilbert and Robert Duncan, to many of the dancers of SF Ballet and some of the singers at SF Opera, all of whom loved him because he was one of the best writers anywhere about serious music, especially opera, ballet, and above all movies, in particular sci fi and film noir, and because almost everything he wrote he wrote out of devotion and gratitude. He was also a serious writer about boxing. He began as a poet, under Duncan's influence in part because both of them came from Bakersfield and both of them had had the same English teacher in high school, Edna Keogh. His critical writing is not so much criticism as it is his intensely lyrical response to an experience of art that he wanted to share. For many years, he wrote for Marinscope and the SF Examiner, long reviews which were not so much reviews as revelations of the way that poetry, at its best, can be revelatory of things otherwise unseen, unheard.

Peter Weltner was raised in suburban New Jersey and piedmont North Carolina, received his A.B. from Hamilton College and his Ph.D. from Indiana University, taught in the English Department of San Francisco State for thirty-seven years, and has published three novels, four collections of short stories, and twenty or so books of poetry, most recently *Sleeper, Waking* (Marrowstone Press, Seattle) and *Crow-Black Stones and a Flock of Crows* (Agenda Editions, UK.) He lives in the Outerlands of San Francisco by the Pacific with his husband of thirty seven years, Atticus Carr. Written after he turned eighty, *A Last Hike In* is his final full length book.

www.ingramcontent.com/pod-product-compliance
Lightning Source LLC
Chambersburg PA
CBHW050857150626
46549CB00013B/2736